a helping hand **Barney**™ *for growing children*

Barney's™
Super Dee Dooper
Treasury

Book of Hugs
What Would Barney Say?
ABC Animals
Count to 10
Color Train
Sing-along Stories: BINGO!
Sing-along Stories: Clean Up!
Sing-along Stories: If You're Happy and You Know It!

SCHOLASTIC INC.

New York   Toronto   London   Auckland   Sydney
Mexico City   New Delhi   Hong Kong   Buenos Aires

Barney's Book of HUGS, ISBN 1-57064-120-X, copyright © 1997 by Lyons Partnership, L.P.
What Would Barney Say?, ISBN 1-57064-121-8, copyright © 1997 by Lyons Partnership, L.P.
Barney's ABC Animals!, ISBN 1-57064-453-5, copyright © 1999 by Lyons Partnership, L.P.
Barney's Count to 10, ISBN 1-58668-249-0, copyright © 1999 by Lyons Partnership, L.P.
Barney's Color Train, ISBN 1-58668-250-4, copyright © 2000 by Lyons Partnership, L.P.
Barney's Sing-along Stories: BINGO, ISBN 1-58668-290-3, copyright © 2002 by Lyons Partnership, L.P.
Barney's Sing-along Stories: Clean Up!, ISBN 0-439-63978-6. First and last verses traditional.
All other verses copyright © 2004 by Lyons Partnership, L.P.
Barney's Sing-along Stories: If You're Happy and You Know It!, ISBN 0-439-45862-5.
First and last verses traditional. All other verses copyright © 2004 by Lyons Partnership, L.P.

12 11 10 9 8 7 6 5 4 3 2 1   5 6 7 8 9 10/0

Printed in Singapore   46
ISBN 0-681-27945-1

First compilation printing, November 2005

Cover illustration by June Valentine-Ruppe

Barney's™ BOOK OF HUGS

Written by
Sheryl Leach and
Patrick Leach

Illustrated by
June Valentine-Ruppe

Or maybe . . .

My favorite hug is a *grandparent hug*.
I love it when they come to visit.

Or maybe . . .

My favorite hug is a *that's OK hug*.
Thank you. That makes me feel better.

Or maybe . . .

Or maybe . . .

Or maybe...

My favorite hug is a *goodnight hug*.
Ah! Now I feel all warm and snuggly.

Or maybe...

My favorite hug is an *I love you hug.*
Awww. That's the best feeling of all!

Hugging once, hugging twice,
Every hug feels very nice.

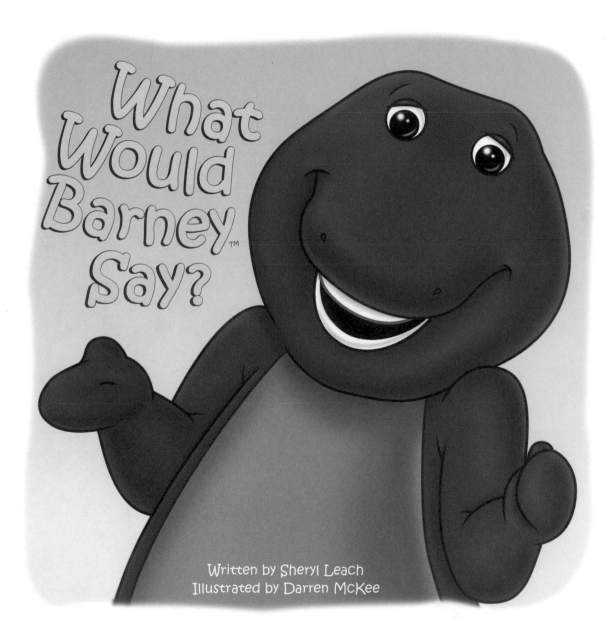

What Would Barney™ Say?

Written by Sheryl Leach
Illustrated by Darren McKee

Barney and BJ were invited to Patrick and Alicia's house to play. "This will be the best day ever," says Patrick. "Thanks for coming over."

What would Barney say?

The four friends made a castle by sharing a giant pile of blocks. They like to play together.

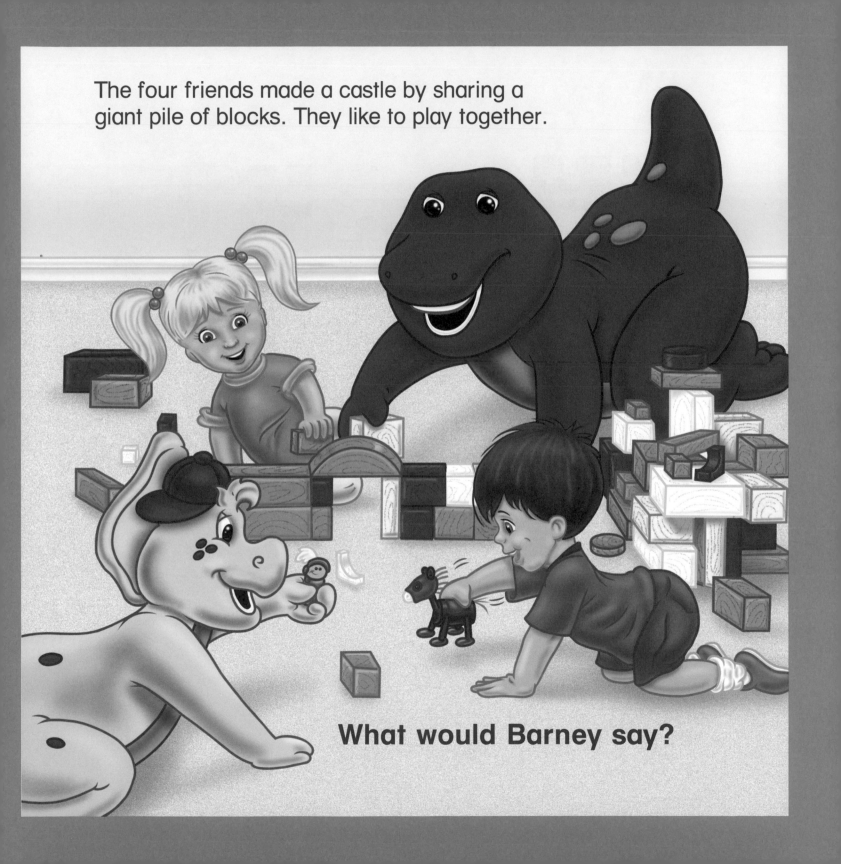

What would Barney say?

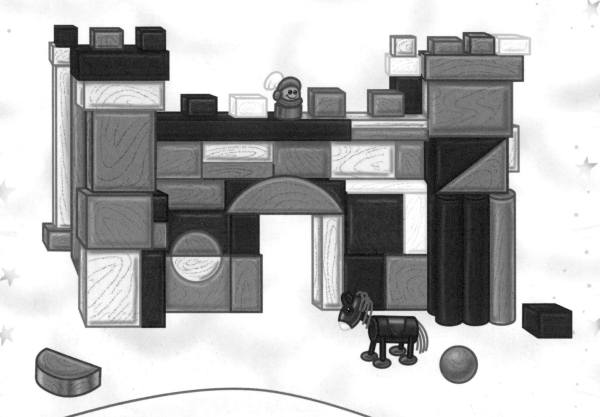

It's great sharing toys.

It's time for a snack. "Uh-oh," says BJ.
"We better wash our hands first."

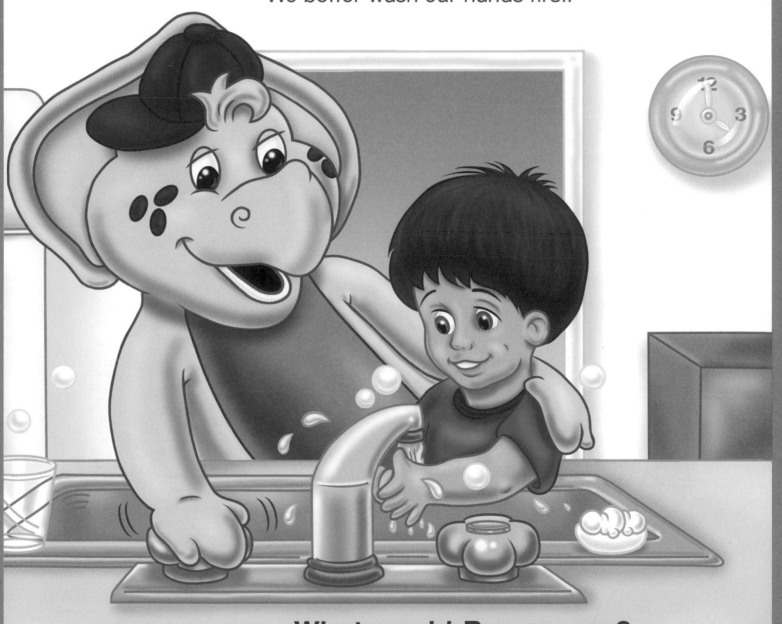

What would Barney say?

Washing your hands before you eat is very important.

What a surprise! Homemade cookies
and a special card for Barney.
"We hope you like the card," says Alicia.

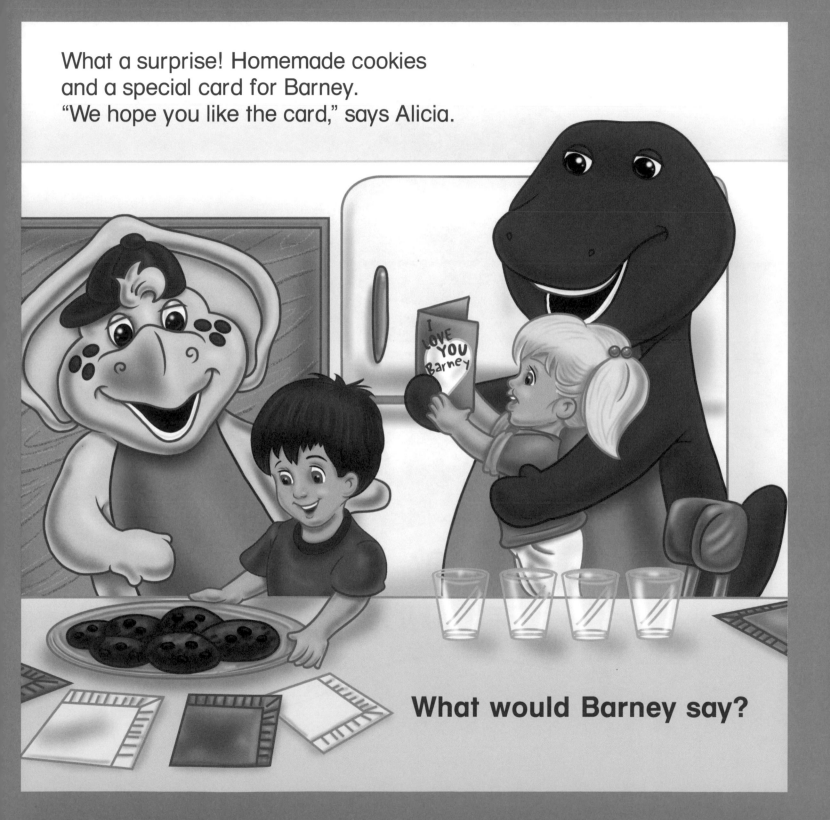

What would Barney say?

Thank you! Thinking of others shows you care.

After eating, everyone helps wash and dry the dishes.
"I always help with the dishes," says Patrick.

What would Barney say?

Cleaning up is
a good thing to do.

Taking turns makes playing more fun.

Patrick and Alicia show Barney and BJ
their favorite books. Story time is
always special.
"Barney, would you like a book to read?"
asks Alicia.

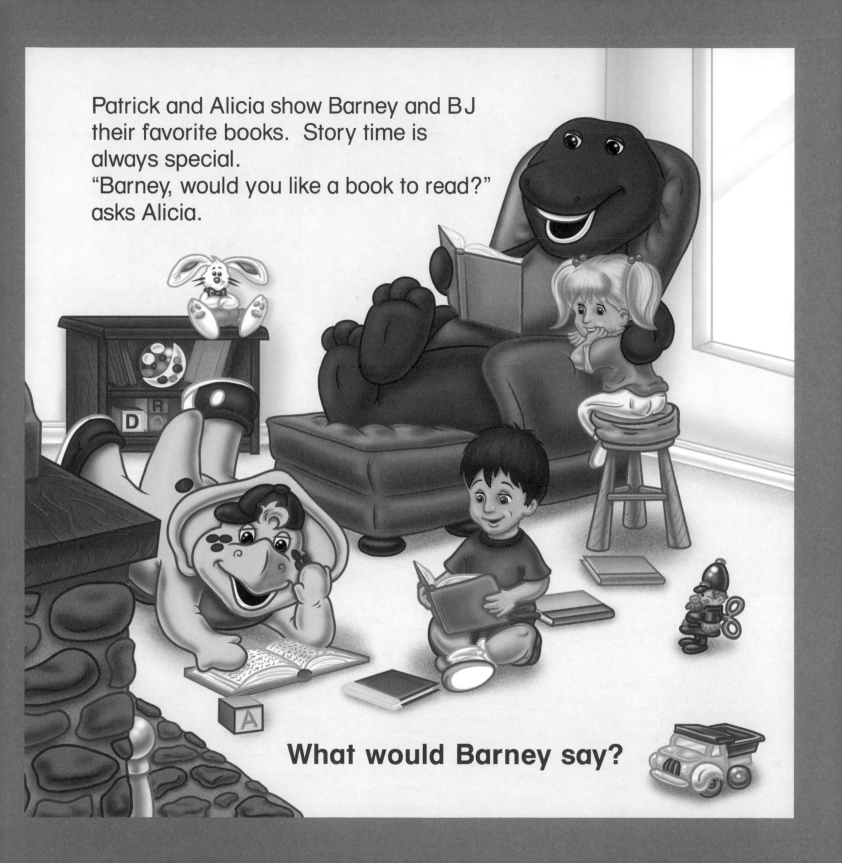

What would Barney say?

Drawing with chalk is a great way to spend the afternoon. "I bet we can draw the biggest jet plane in the world" says Patrick.

What would Barney say?

Anything is possible when you use your imagination.

Friends enjoy walking to the park together. "Look!" exclaims BJ. "The park is just across the street."

STOP

What would Barney say?

Always remember the safety rule—
stop, look both ways, look both ways again,
then cross the street.

Three hugs for Barney!
"Thank you, Barney. This was the best day ever," say BJ, Patrick, and Alicia.

What would Barney say?

Barney's ABC ANIMALS!

Written by Mark S. Bernthal

Illustrated by Darrell Baker

ABCDEFG HIJKLM

I like letters from A, B, C,
All the way to X, Y, Z!
When I count out 1, 2, 3,
Won't you read along with me?

NOPQRS TUVWXYZ

Animals come in every letter.
Would you like to know some better?
We'll take a look at every name.
And play my Animal Alphabet Game.

A

is for **alligator** – her tail is quite long.
She splashes the water while I sing a song.
Her mouth is quite big; if we look underneath,
We'll see rows and rows of pearly white teeth!

B is for **bear,** all fuzzy and brown.
He's gotten quite wet and turned upside-down,
Shaking his body all over to dry.
Now I'm getting soaked from my toes to my eyes!

C is for **cat**. Oh, he does love to sleep!
He can go hours and not make a peep.
He suddenly wakes when he hears "bow-wow-wow,"
And stretches while yawning and saying "meow"!

D is for **dog** — she loves wagging her tail.
And barking at birds that sit on the rail.
And she says "hello" to the birds on the roof
By jumping around and saying "woof-woof."

E is for **eagle**, up in the sky.
He can see everything flying so high.
While watching me wave from down on the ground,
The wind on his wings makes a soft, soaring sound.

F is for **frog**, who sits in a bog,
Out at the end of his favorite log.
He happily greets every bright butterfly,
By shouting "rrrrribbit" as they flutter by!

**G** is for **gorilla**, king of the apes.
He likes to dance as he's eating his grapes.
While jumping about on his favorite stump,
He beats on his chest with a thumpity-thump!

H

is for **hippo** swimming away
In her river home most of the day.
All of her fish friends swim to the side,
Whenever Miss Hippo opens up wide!

I is for **iguana** – she scurries near the ground.
She chases her tail, spinning round and round.
She loves to climb trees that match her color green,
Lounging on a limb, imagining she's queen!

J is for **jaguar,** a spotted jungle cat.
He sat on my basket and nearly squashed it flat.
Although my picnic basket has lots for us to eat,
I hope my jaguar friend will find another seat!

K

is for **kangaroo** who jumps so high!
She looks as though she's ready to fly!
Bouncing up high, she soars like a rocket,
As her baby waves down from her tummy pocket!

L is for **lion**, the animal king.
Whenever I see him, I just want to sing.
Though he wants to join me for one song or more,
Instead of singing softly, he can only roar!

M

is for **mouse** who's always in a hurry.
Running quickly everywhere; oh, how he likes to scurry!
But sometimes he'll stop to sneak a little peek,
And greet his friends around him with a happy squeak.

N

is for **nightingale** sitting in a tree,
Singing for her forest friends sweetly as can be.
Many think the nightingale has the nicest song.
They love to listen to her through the whole day long.

O is for **octopus** who lives in the ocean.
He can move quickly with lots of motion!
I think that swimming with my two legs is great,
But the octopus zips past me, because he has eight!

P is for **porpoise** who wears a happy smile.
She loves to swim around her friends, playing all the while.
But what she likes to do the most is swim quick as a flash
And jump out of the water, landing with a splash!

Q is for **quail** who can hide without fail
In brown-colored grass that matches his tail.
But even though he can be hard to see,
I'll always hear him when he sings to me!

R is for **raccoon**. See the mask on her face?
She likes to be tidy, everything in its place.
Her tail is ringed with many black bands.
And she often likes to wash her very small hands.

S is for **spider,** waving at me.
He's woven a web up in a tree.
Hearing him run through his strands from afar,
Sounds like he's playing a funny guitar!

T is for **turtle** who lives in her shell.
She walks so-o-o-o slowly, but gets around well.
Where she is headed, nobody knows;
But she carries her home wherever she goes!

U

is for **unicorn whale** who has a surprise,
Sitting on his forehead right between his eyes.
His horn is quite handy for pointing at things,
Or playing with me when I toss him these rings!

Y is for **vole** — she's fuzzy and small.
She likes to live in grass that is tall!
A little tunnel is her cozy house.
She squeaks, "Hello" like her cousin the mouse!

W

is for **walrus** — he lives in ice and snow.
The water there is very cold, but he likes it so.
His flippers help him swim quite well, but he hardly walks.
See his two big tusks and listen to him talk!

X is for **X-ray fish** who swim together here.
Isn't it surprising that their bodies are so clear?
They're the most amazing friends I have ever known,
'Cause when I stop and take a look, I can see their bones!

Y is for **yak**, a cousin to the cow.
When I first saw her, I shouted, "Wow!"
Her horns are the same as a cow's, I must say,
But she should get a haircut — and do it right away!

Z is for **zebra**, and one little peek
Tells me he can't really play "hide and seek!"
No matter whatever he hides behind,
His black and white stripes make him easy to find!
(Ready or not . . . here I come!)

Our **ABC** Animals sure have been fun!
I'm happy that now you have met every one.

Barney's
Count to 10

IN   Out

10

Written by Mark S. Bernthal • Illustrated by Darren McKee

Baby Bop laughs and jumps for joy.
We're off to see where they make toys!
BJ's as happy as he can be.
He wants to count the toys we see!
So let's get started right away;
Today's a perfect counting day!

Is that an elephant I see
Walking over here to me?
No! It's Professor Tinkerputt!
I recognize his happy strut!
He makes lots and lots of toys
For all his favorite girls and boys!

1

elephant

Some children want to take a trip
To the moon in a rocket ship.
BJ won't need to go that far—
He's happy here with two toy cars!

2
cars

Squeak!

The factory is so big inside
That Baby Bop can take a ride.
She laughs, she giggles, then she squeals,
"This tricycle has three squeaky wheels!"

3
wheels

Yellow and green, blue and red—
Bright colors flying overhead.
All my friends like to stop and stare,
When I bounce four balls in the air!

4 balls

Professor Tinkerputt's puppet play,
Moves animals in a wiggly way!
It's fun to watch – a real humdinger–
With tiny puppets on each finger!

5

finger puppets

Baby Bop sets the table for tea,
Serving Tinkerputt, BJ and me.
Adding her dolls and a place for herself,
She takes six teacups down from the shelf!

6
teacups

It's always an exciting time
When toys roll down the factory line!
Right behind the new blue dragons,
Here come seven bright red wagons!

7
wagons

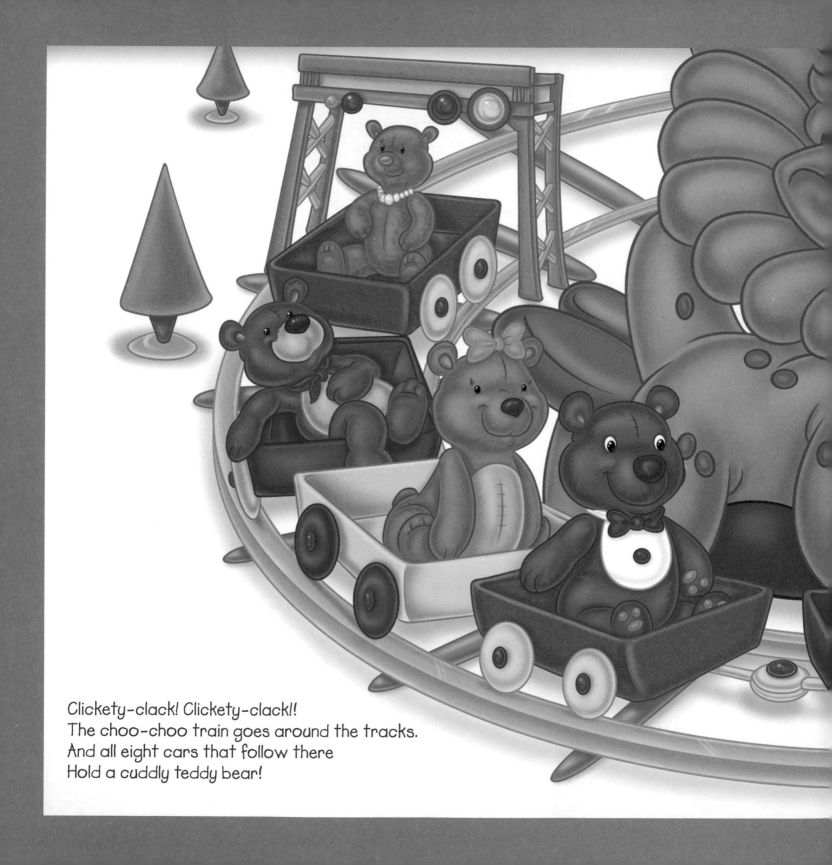

Clickety-clack! Clickety-clack!!
The choo-choo train goes around the tracks.
And all eight cars that follow there
Hold a cuddly teddy bear!

8
teddy bears

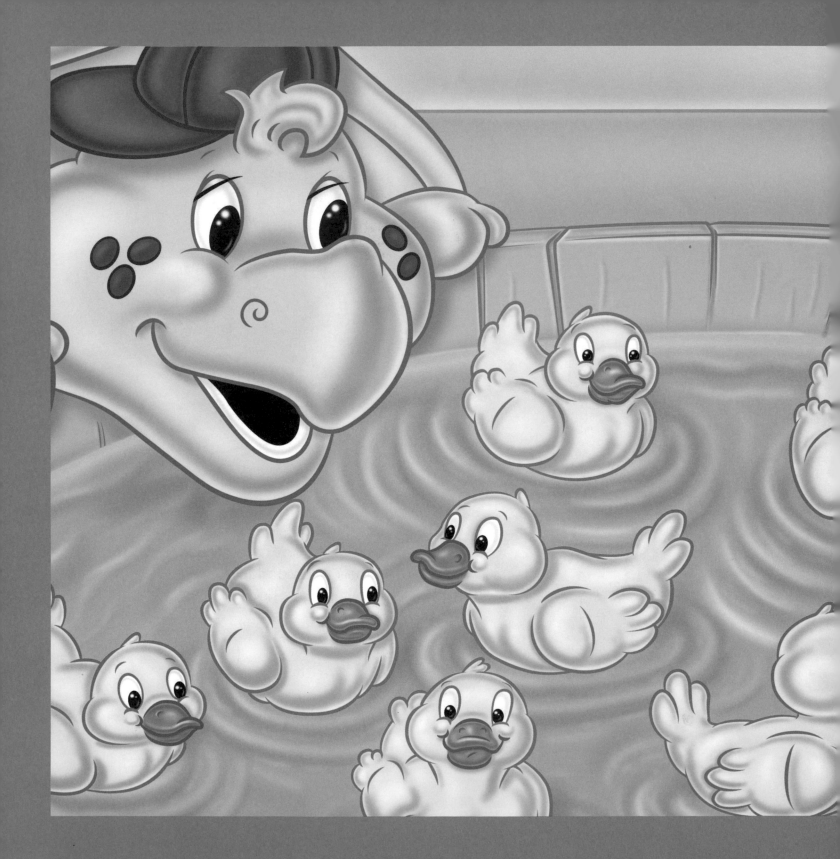

The Professor wants every toy they make
To work just right and never break.
He takes them to a pond to test
Where yellow duckies float their best!

9
ducks

Professor Tinkerputt's cuckoo clock
Passes time with a tickity-tock,
While Baby Bop stacks number blocks
Found inside a painted box!
She starts with one block and ends with ten.
Let's help her count them all again!

10 blocks

Waving goodbye, the day is done.
Counting toys was lots of fun!

Barney's Color Train

Written by Gayla Amaral

Illustrated by Darrell Baker

Clickety-clack, clickety-clack,
The color train chugs down the track!

Clickety-clack, clickety-clack,
The red train car chugs down the track!

Clickety-clack, clickety-clack,
The blue train car chugs down the track!

Ducks that quack and bananas to eat,
Cold lemonade that tastes so sweet,
The bright yellow sun shines in the sky,
As the color train zooms on by.

Clickety-clack, clickety-clack,
The yellow train car chugs down the track.

Clickety-clack, clickety-clack,
The green train car chugs down the tr

Clickety-clack, clickety-clack,
The orange train car chugs down the track!

Clickety-clack, clickety-clack,
The pink train car chugs down the track!

Clickety-clack, clickety-clack,
The brown train car chugs down the track!

Clickety-clack, clickety-clack,
The black train car chugs down the track!

Clickety-clack, clickety-clack,
The purple train car chugs down the track!

Barney's Sing-along Stories

BINGO

Written by Gayla Amaral

Illustrated by Darren McKee

Farmer Barney had a dog
And Bingo was his name, oh.

B-I-N-G-O
B-I-N-G-O
B-I-N-G-O

And Bingo was his name, oh.

Farmer Barney had a dog
And Bingo was his name, oh.

MEOW–I–N–G–O
MEOW–I–N–G–O
MEOW–I–N–G–O

And Bingo was his name, oh.

Farmer Barney had a dog
And Bingo was his name, oh.

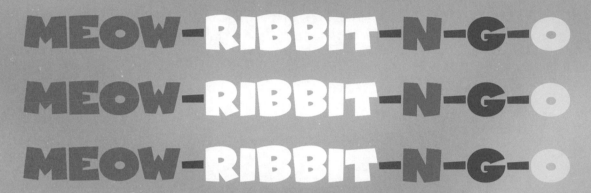

MEOW-RIBBIT-N-G-o
MEOW-RIBBIT-N-G-o
MEOW-RIBBIT-N-G-o

And Bingo was his name, oh.

Farmer Barney had a dog
And Bingo was his name, oh.

MEOW-RIBBIT-QUACK-G-O
MEOW-RIBBIT-QUACK-G-O
MEOW-RIBBIT-QUACK-G-O

And Bingo was his name, oh.

Farmer Barney had a dog
And Bingo was his name, oh.

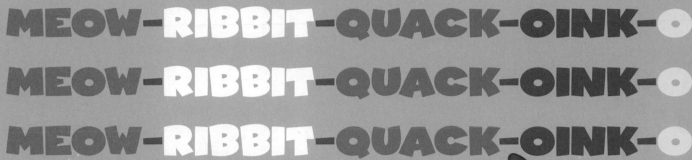

MEOW-**RIBBIT**-QUACK-OINK-o
MEOW-**RIBBIT**-QUACK-OINK-o
MEOW-**RIBBIT**-QUACK-OINK-o

And Bingo was his name, oh.

Farmer Barney had a dog
And Bingo was his name, oh.

To: BINGO
From: Barney

MEOW-RIBBIT-QUACK-OINK-WOOF
MEOW-RIBBIT-QUACK-OINK-WOOF
MEOW-RIBBIT-QUACK-OINK-WOOF

And Bingo was his name, oh.

And Bingo was his name, oh.

Barney's Sing-along Stories

Clean Up!

Adapted by Dena Neusner from traditional lyrics • Illustrated by Darren McKee

Clean up! Clean up!

Everybody everywhere.

Clean up! Clean up!

Everybody do your share!

Clean up! Clean up!
All pet owners everywhere.
Clean up! Clean up!
Scrub and brush and do your share!

Clean up! Clean up!
Garden workers everywhere.
Clean up! Clean up!
Rake it, bag it, do your share!

Clean up! Clean up!
All car washers everywhere.
Clean up! Clean up!
Scrub and shine and do your share!

Clean up! Clean up!

All shopkeepers everywhere.

Clean up! Clean up!

Pick up, sweep up, do your share!

Clean up! Clean up!
Cooks and bakers everywhere.
Clean up! Clean up!
Wipe up, mop up, do your share!

Clean up! Clean up!
Construction workers everywhere.
Clean up! Clean up!
Lift and haul and do your share!

Clean up! Clean up!
Trash recyclers everywhere.

Clean up! Clean up!
Lift it, dump it, do your share!

Clean up! Clean up!
Toys and games are everywhere.
Clean up! Clean up!
Pick up, clean up, do your share!

Clean up! Clean up!
It is bath time everywhere.
Clean up! Clean up!
Wash and rinse and do your share!

Clean up! Clean up!
Everybody everywhere.
Clean up! Clean up!
Everybody do your share!

All clean! Sleep tight.
Thanks for helping
do your share!

Barney's Sing-along Stories

If You're Happy and You Know It!

Adapted from the traditional by Dena Neusner

Illustrated by Darren McKee

If you're happy and you know it,
clap your hands.

If you're happy and you know it,
clap your hands.

If you're happy and you know it,
then your face will surely show it.

If you're happy and you know it,
clap your hands.

If you're happy and you know it,
stomp your feet.

If you're happy and you know it,
stomp your feet.

If you're happy and you know it,
then your face will surely show it.

If you're happy and you know it,
stomp your feet.

If you're happy and you know it,
jump up and down.

If you're happy and you know it,
jump up and down.

If you're happy and you know it,
then your face will surely show it.
If you're happy and you know it,
jump up and down.

If you're happy and you know it,
dance around.

If you're happy and you know it,
dance around.

If you're happy and you know it,
then your face will surely show it.
If you're happy and you know it,
dance around.

If you're happy and you know it,
shout **HOORAY!**
If you're happy and you know it,
shout **HOORAY!**

If you're happy and you know it,
then your face will surely show it.

If you're happy and you know it,
shout **HOORAY!**

If you're happy and you know it,

clap your hands,

stomp your feet,

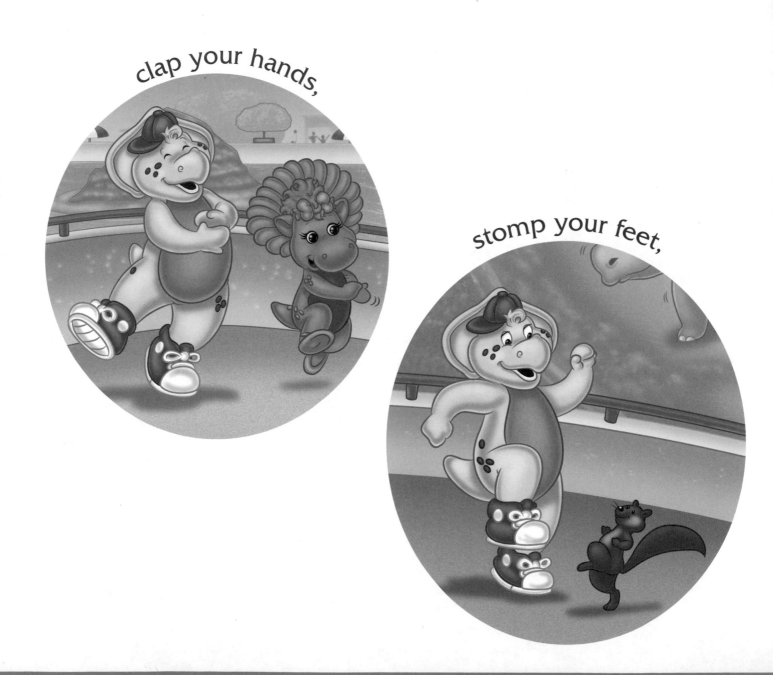

jump up and down,

dance around,

and shout **HOORAY!**